THE GREAT CAT GAME BOOK

To
ELLERY YALE WOOD
in gratitude for her enthusiastic research in her extensive cat library and
collection which made this book possible

First published in Great Britain by Michael Joseph Ltd 1985
44 Bedford Square, London WC1B 3DP

Designed and produced by BELLEW PUBLISHING COMPANY LIMITED,
7 Southampton Place, London WC1A 2DR

British Library Cataloguing in Publication Data.
Bruce, Erika
    The great cat game book.
    1. Games   2. Cats
    I. Title
    790   GV1201
    ISBN 0-7181-2621-1

Printed and bound in Great Britain

The author and publishers wish to record their appreciation of the following persons and organiza-
tions for whose kind assistance they are deeply indebted: Mrs Flora Gill Jacobs, Director of the
Washington Dolls' House and Toy Museum, Dr R. C. Bell, David Drummond, Professor Marco
Fagioli, Professor Enrico Gianfranco, Messrs Guiolio, Enrico, and Guido Giannini, Mrs Mary
Hillier, and Mr Brian Love; also the original publishers of the board games, of which Parker Brothers
Inc. of Salem, Massachusetts still flourishes today; finally, to all those into whose printed material we
delved, especially Cecily M. Rutley and Iona and the late Peter Opie, to whom we must express a
large debt of gratitude.

THE GREAT CAT GAME BOOK

Erika Bruce

Michael Joseph: London

4

CONTENTS

Indoor Games

Outdoor Games

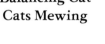

Paws and effect—add aqua and then duck

Louis Wain.

Push-out Cut-outs

Board Games

*Mewsic is one thing,
a little light
caterwauling another
but these sounds
make mother feline edgy.*

INTRODUCTION

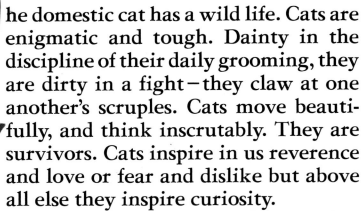

The domestic cat has a wild life. Cats are enigmatic and tough. Dainty in the discipline of their daily grooming, they are dirty in a fight—they claw at one another's scruples. Cats move beautifully, and think inscrutably. They are survivors. Cats inspire in us reverence and love or fear and dislike but above all else they inspire curiosity.

Perhaps it is our puzzlement that has caused us to put them in a multiplicity of games in a variety of cultures down through the centuries. Here we offer indoor and outdoor games, board games—but never games that bore—games of move and counter-move, and games best played in the dark.

Do cats play games? We know that they practise the killing of mice, the capture of birds, and the theft, where possible, of our own supermarket-acquired carrion. But all this is their trade, their work.

Yet we fondly observe cats playing shadow games, lifting ping-pong balls, nudging pens and pencils off tables, and leaping at door handles. On the one hand, we know that with such pranks they perfect their killing craft, but we suspect they also enjoy themselves—just as we enjoy their games.

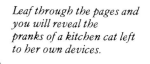

Leaf through the pages and you will reveal the pranks of a kitchen cat left to her own devices.

— INDOOR GAMES —
Cat and Mouse

Cat and Mouse. Who will you be? The velvet-coated Cat has clever, darting paws and wants to pounce on Mouse. Is that you? Mouse is quivering but quick and teases Cat to fury by never getting caught on his claws; perhaps you're Mouse. Use one of the rhymes on page 19 to see who begins as Cat and who as Mouse.

The rest of you must now link hands and form a circle around Mouse to protect her from Cat who even now is scrabbling after her with his paws. Listen how the cunning wretch begins with his slippery questions:

> 'Is the Mouse at home?'
> 'Who wants to know?' answers Mouse.
>   Cat: 'Cat wants to know.'
> Mouse: 'Yes, Mouse is at home.'
>   Cat: 'What o'clock is it?'
> Mouse: 'Time Mouse was gone.'

Now the chase begins. Cat can try anything. 'Protect me,' cries Mouse. Sometimes Cat breaks into the circle only to find that Mouse has fled to the outside. If that happens Cat must remember the rule that says he should pad around the inside miaowing. If he forgets he must not be let out. Cat trapped. Mouse has won. If Cat catches Mouse then Mouse becomes Cat and a new mouse is chosen.

Or try the game this way. Everyone except Cat and Mouse sits on the floor in two rows facing each other. Cat and Mouse are at opposite sides of the room. One row of you supports Cat, the other protects Mouse. To make it more like life Cat and Mouse are blindfolded. Cat's friends and Mouse's guardians may not move; they can only advise as Cat and Mouse stumble around the room: 'You are near Mouse' or 'Mouse, beware Cat is to your right.' The game ends when Mouse is caught, only to begin again with a new mouse.

The age-old-chase: the round hand held game has two artful mice with two galloping cats in hot pursuit. Their only hope is to squeak into mouse-sized shelters. The magic lantern slide above lays unfair odds: it's two to one now.

The oldest game known to cat:
Cat and Mouse.
See what happens; flick these pages quickly

Hiss Puss

Here is a crafty game: *Hiss Puss.* Please sit in a circle. You know one another's first names? Good. Now, in alphabetical order – Alison, Archibald, Andromeda, Arthur – each player calls a number. The first one calls 'one', the second 'two' and so on. Easy. Ah, but when you reach 'five' and any multiple of 'five' (10, 15, 20 etc.) instead of saying the number you must let out a truly terrifying hiss. 'One', 'two', 'three', 'four', '*hiss*', 'six', 'seven'... Seven? Whenever you come to 'seven' and any of its multiples (14, 21, 28), you must not say that number but say *puss* as creamily as you can. Again, 'one', 'two', 'three', 'four', '*hiss*', 'six', '*puss*'... And when you come to a number such as thirty-five which is a multiple of 'five' and 'seven' what do you do? Right. You go '*hiss-puss*'. If you miss a hiss or a puss or a hiss-puss you drop out. Last Cat still in the game WINS.

Chitterbob

You are not to laugh. Sit in a circle and one of you hold a stick or pencil in your hand and repeat after me:

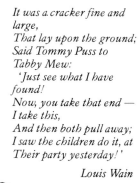

> There was a man and his name was Cob;
> He had a wife and her name was Mob;
> She had a cat, and her name was Chitterbob.
> Chitterbob says Mob;
> Mob's cat was Chitterbob;
> Cob, Mob and Chitterbob.

No laughing. Be Cat-like. Be catatonic. Hand the stick on to the next player who must now repeat the rhyme with no mistakes and no giggles. And now the next player, and the next.
Anyone who laughs is out of the game and has to pay a forfeit (see page 23) or recite this rhyme:

> No last nicht but the nicht afore,
> Three black cats com' roaring at the door;
> One got whisky, one got rum,
> And one got the dish-clout o'er his bum.

The most serious player
WINS the game.

It was a cracker fine and large,
That lay upon the ground;
Said Tommy Puss to Tabby Mew:
'Just see what I have found!
Now, you take that end —
I take this,
And then both pull away;
I saw the children do it, at Their party yesterday!'

Louis Wain

The Parson's Cat

Everyone sits around a table. The first player exclaims, 'The Parson's Cat is an ambitious cat!' Not to be outdone, the next player says, 'The Parson's Cat is an ambitious, affable cat.' The third player says, 'The Parson's Cat is an ambitious, affable, ancient cat.' And so on. The first person who cannot think of a new adjective beginning with 'a' drops out. A new round begins with 'b' – puss could be big, bulbous, bulging, barmy, brilliant... The winner is the last person in the game. If there are twenty-seven of you the game goes all the way to Zzzz.

What is my Thought Like?

Question time. 'How can my cat be like a table?' you ask the person sitting next to you. 'Because both have four legs,' she answers. She then asks the person sitting next to her, 'Why is my cat like Abraham Lincoln?' The answer is probably, 'because both have whiskers.' 'How can my cat be like a saint?' The first person who cannot think of an answer to a 'How can my cat be like' question drops out. The game continues until only one player remains.

Naturally I am frilled to be here but what I say is, if you've got it, flaunt it.

Let the Cat out of the Bag

Were you the first person to drop out in the last game? Then please step outside the room for a moment, the rest of us must confer. We must agree a word. We will each include this word in the answers to the questions which will be asked of us individually when the player returns to the room. He can and should ask what he likes. We must each take care to disguise our agreed word. Suppose we choose 'care' as our word. The questioner could ask, 'Did you see Disneyland last summer?' 'Oh no, we lost all our maps and did not care to get lost ourselves.' 'Do you eat peas off your knife?' the questioner might ask your neighbour. 'Oh no,' says your neighbour. 'Too many peas are lost if you do not take care to balance them properly.' This goes on until the questioner guesses the word. The person who lets the cat out of the bag with the answer must then become the new questioner.

Is this my cue for a little side bet?

The Pretty, Playful, Tortoiseshell Cat

For this game one of us must become a treasurer – we can choose by using one of the counting-out rhymes on page 19. The Treasurer takes an object and imperiously (as treasurers are wont to be) commands his neighbour to the left, 'Take this!' This second player naturally asks, 'What's this?' and the Treasurer's surprising reply is, 'A pretty playful Tortoiseshell Cat.' The second person passes the object to the neighbour on his left and the words are repeated, and so on. When the object finds its way back into the Treasurer's hands the Treasurer starts off again, but this time he adds one of the lines below. The first of these lines is 'Two Cows, each in a hat.' So the Treasurer passes the object to the left, 'Take this!' and his neighbour asks, 'What's this?' and the reply is, 'Two Cows, each in a hat. With a pretty playful Tortoiseshell Cat.' Round we go again. On the third round the Treasurer introduces the line 'Three Tigers...' and so on until eventually all the players are reciting the rhyme in turn. Anyone who blunders, and this includes the Treasurer, must pay a forfeit (see page 23).

Command.—Take this.

Question.—What's this ?

Answer.

A pretty, playful, tortoise-shell Cat.

*The original game,
with 14 colour engravings,
published by
D. Carvalho, London*

*A French version of
Puss in Boots –
Le Chat Botté – produced
in roller form
for shadow – theatre shows*

Twelve Cocks, with cambric
kerchiefs white,
Lamenting that all is not right;
  Sobbing, sighing, moaning,
crying,
  That Britain's glories all are
dying.

Eleven Greyhounds in a boat,
  Tow'd up the river by a Goat.

Ten Lobsters in a dish
  So fresh as any heart can wish.

Nine Beetles against the wall
  Close by an old woman's apple
store.

Eight wise Kittens, busy all,
  Sorting silver, large and small;
On their sagacity depend,

And to the Bank your silver
send.

Seven Bears with gloomy looks,
  Making up their yearly books,
With bad debts fill'd and other
losses;
Sure never Bears meet with such
crosses.

Six Barbers dressing wigs,
  For a dozen learned Pigs.

Five Hens going to France
  To learn a fashionable dance.

Four Hares making a mat.
  Three Tigers catching a Rat,
Two Cows, each in a hat
  With a pretty, playful,
Tortoiseshell Cat.

Mariage du Marquis de Carabas avec la fille du Roi.   *Mais l'Ogre est dévoré dès qu'il se transforme en souris.*   *L'Ogre changé en lion effraye le Chat Botté.*

Puss in the Corner

One of us must stand in the centre of the room and the rest will lurk in the corners and behind pieces of furniture. 'Poor Puss wants a corner,' cries the player in the centre, or, if she wishes, she wails, 'Poor Puss, give me a drop of milk.' This is the signal for change – everyone must change places calling 'Puss, Puss, Puss' to each other in order to attract one another's attention. The player in the centre will try to find a place in a corner or behind a piece of furniture. The person left without a place goes into the centre of the room.

A little wallflower, fan in paw, hopes for a dance at the SophistiCats' party. Younger pusses try lucky dip in a bran tub

Pussy wants a Corner

The players outnumber the corners and hiding places by one but everyone begins in the middle of the room and then rushes from the centre to find a place of hiding at the edge. The slowest is Pussy. Pussy must call on each player in turn, plaintively mewing, 'Pussy wants a corner.' 'Ask my neighbour,' each replies as Pussy passes on. But the player Pussy has just left must try to exchange places with his neighbour and Pussy can pounce and try to slip into one of the empty spaces. Pussy must continue until she is quick enough to dart in. The player who loses his place becomes Pussy.

Finger Shadow Plays

Fat cats, well-fed cats are indolent. This game is for them. All you have to do is raise your hands and make shadows on the wall. You need a good light to cast a shadow. Indolent extroverts can make animal

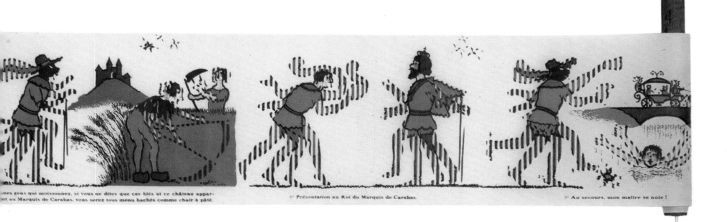

noises and sing songs to accompany the creatures they make from the shadows. Try the rhymes below; make the shape of five little mice and the wise old cat. Good at animal sounds are you? Then let's have a rendition of 'When Cats Get Up.'

MICE ON THE SHELF

A PIE

Five little mice on the shelf up high,
Feasting so daintily on a pie —

'How mischievous you are,'
Cried Mother Pussycat,
'To take your Mother's thread,
To play a game like that.'
'We're busy, mother dear,'
The little pussies said,
'Making a cat's cradle
For Baby Pussy's bed.'

When cats get up in the morning
   They always say Good day,
When cats get up in the morning,
   They always say Good day,
Miaow! miaow! miaow! miaow!
   That is what they say,
They say, Miaow! miaow!
   Miaow! miaow! that is what they say.

●

When dogs get up, etc.
  Bow-wow! bow-wow! etc.
●
When pigs get up, etc.
  Grunt! grunt! etc.

When hens get up, etc.
  Cluck! cluck! etc.
●
When ducks get up, etc.
  Quack! quack! etc.
●
When geese get up, etc.
  Hiss! hiss! etc.
●
When donkeys get up, etc.
  Hee-haw! hee-haw! etc.
●
When we get up, etc.
  Good Day! good day! etc.

Mew

One of us is blindfolded; the rest will sit on chairs. Up and down the line walks the blindfolded player and then sits on someone's lap. 'Mew,' she says. 'Mew,' replies the person on whose lap she is sitting. From this 'mew' the blindfolded person tries to guess in whose lap she has landed. Should she guess wrongly then the players change places and she must try again. If she is right then the player upon whom she has sat receives the blindfold.

Cat after Mouse

There are many versions of this ancient – and adult – game (it is also known as *Threading the Needle*). In this version the players, except one, form a ring with the extra player outside the ring. This extra player is Mouse. Mouse runs swiftly around the ring and tugs gently at the clothes of one of the players in the ring. Alarm! That player becomes Cat. Cat gives chase to Mouse. Where Mouse goes Cat must follow, inside or outside the ring, under the players' arms, in and around the ring. When Mouse is caught he or she takes the space in the ring left by Cat, and Cat becomes Mouse. The new Mouse then chooses another Cat and the cycle begins anew – catch as Cats can; Mouse, make haste.

Another version of this game has two players raising their arms and making an arch through which the rest of the players file two by two. As the last couple walk beneath the arch they then form the arch. In other versions the two players forming the arch come down to enclose a couple of players. In most versions rhymes or songs are chanted as the players march around.

The Lucky Ringtail Cat puzzle was produced by R. Journet & Co., London, with the dazzling claim: 'Popular Portable Puzzles Proving Positively Perplexing and Perpetually Pleasing Posers Presenting Persistently Provoking Problems Providing Profuse Pleasure, and Producing a Palliative or Placid Panacea to People Possessing a Propensity for Persistence, Patience, Perspicacity and Painstaking Propensities'

There's a similar game to this Jolly Bowling Game, the Three Little Kittens on page 29 which you can easily make yourself. Go on, play for high stakes

Conundrums

Pause for breath after your physical exertions in the energetic feline games of the preceding pages and bend your mind to some silly riddles and conundrums. Riddling is a time-honoured pastime which has absorbed scholars, wits, jesters and fools from the beginning of history. Present these cat word games to the losers of any of the games in the book to confound them further.

*Puss-in-Boots,
swashbuckling
and masterful, is off to
London Town*

1 Why is a cat biting her tail
like a good economist?
•

2 Who was it had a pussy cat,
And sent it out o'er the
sea,
And then became Lord
Mayor, they said,
And rich as rich can be?
•

3 Why do you think a cat's tail
resembles happiness?
•

4 As I was going to St Ives,
I chanced to meet with
nine old wives;
Each wife had nine sacks;
Each sack had nine cats;
Each cat had nine kits;
Kits, Cats, Sacks, and Wives,
Tell me how many were
going to St Ives?
•

5 Why is it that a schoolmaster
and his pupil
lead a cat and dog life?
•

6 Why is a cat like a gossiping
person?
•

7 If you pull my cat's tail,
why is it like a teapot?
•

8 It has a head like a cat,
feet like a cat, a tail
like a cat, but it is not
a cat.
What is it?
•

9 Furry, Furry, ginger or
tabby,
My coat is never shabby,
Sleekly shines this coat of
hairs
As I wash behind my ears.
What am I?
•

10 Why can a cat never expect
a fishmonger to be
generous?
•

ANSWERS

1 Because she makes both ends meet!
2 Dick Whittington.
3 Because run after it as much as she can, she cannot catch it.
4 Only myself. I was going to St Ives, but all the others were coming back.
5 Because the master belongs to the canin' (canine) species and the pupil to the feelin' (feline) species.
6 Because it is a tail-bearer (tale-bearer).
7 Because you're teasing it (your-tea-is-in-it).
8 A kitten.
9 A cat.
10 Because his business makes him sell fish (selfish).

A change of pace, here is a tongue-twister:

'The cat ran over the roof with a lump of raw liver,'

Whoever says it the fastest five times over, without a slip, gets first chance to present the limericks to the assembled party – with mime, too! Gather round, gather round...

Limericks

These limericks are all clean because they've been vetted for publication. Cries of 'shame!' But wait, you'll find that the American Society of Limerickers and the British Museum's Limericks books have a 'For Adults Only' collection. Make up your own with each of you adding a line in turn.

There was a young kitten called Sox,
  Who was cunning and quick as a fox.
She ate rather a lot,
  And danced the fox-trot,
That clever young kitten called Sox.

●

There once was a puss called Biuaz,
  Who had plenty of Razzmataz.
When they asked, 'What d'you like?'
  She said, 'Turkish Delight',
That fluffy Turk called Biuaz.

●

There once was a tomcat named
  Rex,
Who only liked kippers and sex.
  He went on the tiles,
Disturbed cats for miles,
  That naughty young tomcat
named Rex.

A musical tomcat named Miles,
  Earned a few boots on the tiles,
But now he makes twiddle,
  Strung up on a fiddle,
That miserable tomcat named
  Miles.

Latin Nonsense

The Victorians loved these 'Latin' nonsense rhymes. This one, written in 1846, tells the tale of Felis who was not an academic cat. And, since it is once again fashionable for every tale to have a moral tail to it, you may learn something here – see the last verse.

Felis sedit by a hole.
Intentus he, cum omni soul,
Prendere rats.
Mice cucurrunt trans the floor
In numero duo, tres, or more
Obliti cats.

Felis saw them oculis;
'I'll have them,' inquit he, 'I guess,
'Dum ludunt.'
Tunc ille crept towards the group;
'Habeam,' dixit, 'good rat soup –
'Pingues sunt.'

Mice continued all ludere;
Intenti they in ludum vere
Gaudenter.
Tunc rushed the felis into them,
Et tore them omnes limb from limb
Violenter.

Mures omnes, nunc be shy,
Et aurem proebe mihi
Benigne.
Sit hoc satis – 'verbum sat' –
Avoid a whopping big tomcat
Studiose.

Tommy Brown

If you listen carefully to the mews and miaows in this game you will win it. In this game of hide and seek one player chooses an object and hides it. But do not use a real cat as your hidden object – it will only wander off in the middle of the game. Anyway, once the object has been hidden the rest of you will look for it, chanting as you go:

We lost our cat a week ago,
  But can't tell where to find it.
We sometimes hear a tuneful noise,
  It's daily growing weaker.
So Tommy Brown we all must say,
  That you are the seeker.

Whenever one of you comes close to where the object is hidden the person who hid it will mew and miaow loudly but sadly. If you look in the wrong place or move from the right one, the mews will grow weak and most pitiful. Whoever finds the object gets to hide it in the next round. You can also introduce prizes or allow the person who has hidden the object three chances to cheat.

There is a rat hidden on the person of Major-General Cat below. Find rat

This is Major-General Cat: See if you can find the rat?

The Knight Series. NO. 849.

THE PUZZLE CARDS.
PUBLISHED BY, ARRANGEMENT
WITH DEAN & SON, L.TD LONDON.

Balancing Cat

A cat can pause on a wire, balancing itself in the breeze. A cat will always land upright. Cats can probably balance other cats on their tails. Cats balance to perfection. Make your own balancing cat with card, scissors, colour pencils and a paperclip. Draw the cat as shown below on a piece of paper, transfer the drawing to a piece of card, and cut it out. The four paws should balance on the edge of something like a pencil so that the tail swings freely. Check the tail does swing, weighting it with a paperclip. Colour in the markings and eyes, whiskers, nose and mouth.

*The Great Gatto Brothers
—maestros of the
high wire, liquid masters
of effortless balance*

Cats Mewing

O ne of us will be blindfolded and the rest will move quietly and cat-like in a circle around him. The blindfolded person will reach out and touch one of the silently padding players. The player thus touched must now mew like a cat caught out but cleverly disguising his voice. If the blindfolded hunter cannot guess his prey's name then he must release him and try again. When eventually he succeeds in capturing someone he recognizes, the prey becomes the hunter and the game continues. According to the kind of party you are having, the hunter can be rewarded with a prize or the prey penalized with a forfeit.

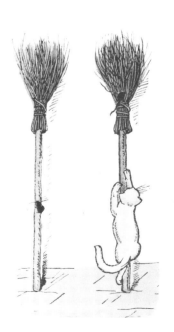

Catsequences

atsequences is a furry version of the well-known *Consequences.* You all need paper and pencil; and each of you writes the name of a famous cat (1) and folds the paper over so that no one else can see what is written. Pass the piece of paper on to the player on your left who will write another name, either of a cat or a person (2). Fold the paper again and pass it on. This time you each write down an action that took place (3) – fold and pass on. Then write down the place (4) – fold, pass on. Then the reason for the incident (5). Fold, pass on; add the opinion of the world (6) and then, finally, the Catsequence (7). You'll end up with something like this:

1 Puss in Boots and
2 The King of France
3 Went skuba diving
4 Outside Grand Central Station
5 Because the fruit was not ripe
6 The world thought the time was right for it
7 The Catsequences were that the Japanese took to gum in a big way

And the catsequences were that she joined the Salvation Army

OUTDOOR GAMES
Rhymes and Chants

All the rhymes and chants on these pages, some dating back to the century before last, can be used for parlour games or outdoor games. Children recite them outdoors while they are playing hopscotch or at the turn of a skipping rope, for example. The rhymes and chants are also used as counting-out chants, like eenie-meenie-miney-mo, to determine who goes first in any of the games in the book. If you feel energetic after a summer barbecue, introduce your friends to some of the outdoor games on pages 20-22.

Ding, Dong, Bell,
  Pussy's in the well.
Who put her in?
  Little Johnny Green.
Who pulled her out?
  Little Tommy Stout.
●

Ding Dong Bell, poor Pussie has
  fall'n i' th' well.
Who threw her in? Little Tom
  O'Linne,
What a naughty boy was that
  To drown poor Pussie cat,
That never did him any harm,
  But catch'd a mouse i' th' barn.
●

Rat-a-tat-tat, who is that?
  Only grandma's pussy-cat,
What do you want?
  A pint of milk.
Where is your money?
  In my pocket;
Where is your pocket?
  I forgot it.
Oh, you silly pussy-cat.
●

Out goes the rat,
  Out goes the cat,
Out goes the lady
  With the big green hat.
Y.O.U. spells you,
  O.U.T. spells out.
●

The story of *That Little Black Cat*
was written by D'Arcy Wentworth Thomson
in the early 1860s:

  'Who's that ringing at our doorbell?'
    'I'm a little black cat, and I'm not very well.'
  'Then you rub your little nose with a little mutton-fat
    'And that's the best cure for a little pussy-cat.'
●

Many different versions exist of these
rhymes, with local variations appear-
ing through the centuries. This one's
dated at 1740:

  Cheitie Pussie
    Catch a moosie
  Rinnin through
    Her little hoosie.

And one more counting-out chant:

  Hiddlety, diddlety, dumpty,
    The cat ran up the plum tree.
  Half a crown to fetch her down,
    Hiddlety, diddlety, dumpty.
●

The two gray Kits
And the gray Kits' mother
All went over
The bridge together.
The bridge broke down,
They all fell in,
'May the rats
Go with you,'
Says Tom Bolin.
(Eleanor W. Talbot, 1882)

Cat

Mr Punch must have been hit in the eye with a cat when he wrote, 'This mania for playing at Cat is no less absurd than dangerous, for it is a game which apparently has no other aim than the windows of houses and the heads of the passers-by.' (*Punch*, 23 April 1853)

We need two players or two teams; a stout stick for clouting the Cat with; a Cat – a small piece of wood; and a circle drawn on the ground.

One player throws the Cat at the circle, the other defends the circle with the stick. Then what? If the Cat gets in the circle the batsman is OUT. If not, the batsman clouts the Cat as far away as he can. If the other player catches the Cat as it flies through the air, the batsman is out. If not, then the batsman has scored points. How many? That depends how far the Cat went. Measure the distance in strides – one stride equals one point.

But there is a twist in the tail. When the batsman has hit the Cat, the pitcher *offers* the batsman a number of points: 'That's worth fifteen points.' 'Nope, I want more.' 'Twenty?' 'No.' 'Twenty-five?' 'Done.' The game continues. But if the batsman refuses the pitcher's final offer the pitcher must measure the distance. If the distance is less than his final offer then the batsman loses all those points. If the pitcher underestimated then the batsman gets the number of points that the pitcher measured.

A·CAT·CAME·FIDDLING·OUT·OF·A
BARN,
WITH·A·PAIR·OF·BAGPIPES·UNDER
HER·ARM;
SHE·COULD·SING·NOTHING·BUT
FIDDLE·DE·DEE,
THE·MOUSE·HAS·MARRIED·THE
HUMBLE·BEE;
PIPE, CAT — DANCE, MOUSE,—
WE'LL·HAVE·A·WEDDING·AT·OUR
GOOD·HOUSE.

*When Tom first went to school he was
Up in a blanket tossed;
He shook and shivered in his fright,
And thought his breath was lost.
He screamed as up on high he flew,
A dreadful noise he made,
The other cats all laughed at him
Because he was afraid.
But now he's been at school a year,
When tossing's to be done,
He holds the corner of his sheet
And thinks it splendid fun.*

Cathole

Do not attempt this game if you have a lush green lawn. Dig a hole in the ground. One player will defend this hole with a stick thrust into it as another player lobs a ball into it. Ball in the hole and the batsman is out; the bowler becomes the batsman. *Or*: place a stone on the ground. From five yards away a bowler will throw a ball at the stone, which will be defended by a batsman with his stick or bat. If the ball is hit and the bowler or some other member of the opposing team does not catch it (in which case the batsman is OUT) then the batsman will run to and fro between the stone and the bowler's mark, scoring runs. Meanwhile the bowler or his fielders will be retrieving the ball. If they get the ball to the stone before the batsman is in his place defending it, the batsman has been run out.

Cat i' the Hole

Please do not try to read these instructions unless your mind is clear – they could make your head reel. Ready? Then we will begin. You need a ball. You also need a number of holes and sticks – if there are seven of you playing then you'll need six holes and six sticks; if there are eight of you then seven holes and seven sticks. You see? Let us suppose there are seven of you: six of you each stand beside a hole (with each hole an equal distance from the others). Each player has a stick which he puts in the

hole. Player number seven takes the ball. When he gives the word all the players must change places, taking their sticks with them. While the six are madly trying to change places the person with the ball tries to seize a hole for himself and drop his ball into it. The player who does not find a place is OUT and takes the ball in the next round.

Hiss, spit, kick – the Paw-Ball Match for hairy hooligans

Cat and Mouse

So we have the CAT team and the MOUSE team, each in its own camp. Halfway between the two camps there is a peg in the ground and attached to this is one short length of cord and one long length of cord. Each camp sends a person out to the middle – one is Cat, the other Mouse. Both are blindfolded. The long cord is given to Cat and the short to Mouse. Cat must catch Mouse and they must not let go of their cords. The two camps advise their respective warriors – mewing and squeaking their warnings and encouragement. Set a time limit. If Cat has not eaten Mouse in five minutes then Mouse has WON. Play on until every person in the camps has 'had a go'.

And here it's one to one – splat!

Cat Tiggy

Why do birds perch in trees and atop the roof tops? To keep out of Cat's paws, of course. Now we too are in pursuit of perches. We form a circle and someone cries, 'The last perched is It!' and we all scramble like fury to find somewhere off the ground. The last person to find a perch is It, the Cat. Cat will catch you if Cat can. You may try changing perches but then Cat will try to capture you. If you are caught you become Cat. It will then occur to your clever cat-like brain to catch the former Cat who caught you before he has had a chance to perch. Not allowed. You must not catch the old cat until he or she has perched once.

Cudgel

Have you ever thought, when playing a team ball game, that it would be fun to steal off with the ball and hide it?

Four or more people can play in two teams. Make two holes ten feet apart. Etch a circle one foot in diameter around each hole. Give two batsmen a stick each and tell them to choose a hole and stick their stick in it. The other two are bowlers (one per hole) standing behind the batsman. The two bowlers are opposing the two batsmen. One bowler throws a Cat (a small piece of wood) and tries to get it into the batsman's hole at the farther end.

If the batsman keeps the Cat out with the stick he runs to change places with his partner and scores one point. If the Cat falls not in the hole but the circle, something odd occurs. The bowler retrieves the Cat and both bowlers walk away into a huddle where one of them hides the Cat on his person. Then they both return to the holes.

The batsmen then leave their holes, leaving a stick in each hole, and go into a huddle to decide which of the bowlers has the Cat. Having made their guess one of them races off, collects his stick and puts it in the hole nearest the bowler whom he believes has the Cat.

Meanwhile the other batsman runs off to the other hole. If the batsmen have guessed right, the bowler with the Cat throws it to the opposite

"Oft in the stilly night."

You ought to see the other fellow

Pause for thought as the cat reflects on the laws of Newton and awaits the crash.

Defiant to the last, the furry feline is still ferocious to behold

bowler for him to lodge it into the hole before the second batsman can reach it. If the batsmen were wrong in their guess the bowler with the Cat puts it in the hole as soon as the batsman has started to run. The two bowlers then become batsmen in the next game. If the batsmen leave their holes without a stick then the bowlers can get them out simply by dropping the Cat in one of the holes. If there are several players these can be used as fielders – picking up the Cat as soon as it has been hit and getting it to the nearest undefended hole.

Forfeits

If you decide that the loser in any of the games is to be penalized, choose one of the following forfeits.

● You must put your cat into the next room without opening the door or the window.

> All you have to do is write your cat's name on a piece of paper and slide it through the keyhole.

● Describe your cat without using the words 'and', 'I' and 'it'.

● Kiss your own shadow without laughing.

● Approach each corner of the room and recite:

> A,B,C, Catch the Cat by the knee
>> L,M,N,O, let the poor thing go.

● What is in a cat but not in a kitten? It is a conundrum, yet not a riddle.

> The letter C.

● Perform for other players:

> Knock, Knock.
>> Who's there?
> Ammonia.
>> Ammonia who?
> Ammonia little cat who can't reach the doorbell.

● Do a purrfect Cat's Cradle.

● Say this tongue-twister very quickly twenty times:

Patty Pettingposh patted her cat Patsy, did Patty Pettingposh.

● Answer the riddle:

> Paddy went out, and his cat went with him.
>> The cat did not walk in front of him, not behind him,
> Nor on one side of him.
>> Where did the cat walk?
> On the other side.

The Cats' Chorus: whoever pays the forfeit sings one song, while all the other players sing a different song. Oh, cacophony!

PUSH-OUT CUT-OUTS

We invite you here to exercise your skills as a model-maker. Each of the models in this section is, of course, intended to be played with and each is centuries old in origin. Do take care to make the models as robustly as you can, reinforcing joins with transparent tape or glue. If at any point you are uncertain about the instructions study the illustrations. Be as cat-like as you can — fastidious and dextrous — and keep your paws clean. Good Luck.

Gare au Matou

HOW TO ASSEMBLE

1 Push out plinth A. Push out circle B and throw it away. Push out C and keep it. Fold the flaps on A into right angles and glue into position using the tabs at each corner. You have now a square plinth with a hole.

2 Push out D and E and make into plinths. Take plinth D and poke out 'x' with a matchstick. Leave matchstick in place, this is now a *spindle*.

3 Push out F and push it on to the *spindle* so that it rests on plinth D. Glue. Push plinth E on top of F. Thus the disc F is sandwiched on a spindle between D and E. OK?

4 Push out G and H and curl each piece around a knife blade to make them into arches. Fold their tabs into right angles.

5 Take circle C and take G. Insert tab 1 into slit 1.

6 Now fix the unit C, G, H to the plinth A by pushing the remaining tabs on G, H through slits 2, 3, 4 on plinth. Glue in position. Make sure circle C is level with the top of plinth A.

7 You now have a unit made up of plinth A and C, G, H. Place it on top of the spindle and circle F — the whole assembly should look like the model illustrated and you should be able to twirl the spindle, and circle F should spin freely inside plinth A. Yes? Good.

One more thing: press out I and J, curl them into arches and glue into place as shown in the picture.

HOW TO PLAY

1 Any number of people can play.

2 Each player decides if he is the black or the white mouse; having decided, he turns the spindle and:

3 If the mouse stops in front of the cat, the cat eats it up and the player is out.

4 Should the mouse stop at the sack of corn or at the bread, the player loses 5 points.

5 If the mouse stops at the mousehole the player has two more turns.

6 If the mouse comes to rest at the mouse-trap the player misses as many turns as it takes the next player to catch up with him.

7 The mouse that stops under the arch gains 5 points.

8 The winner is the person who is first to reach 100 points.

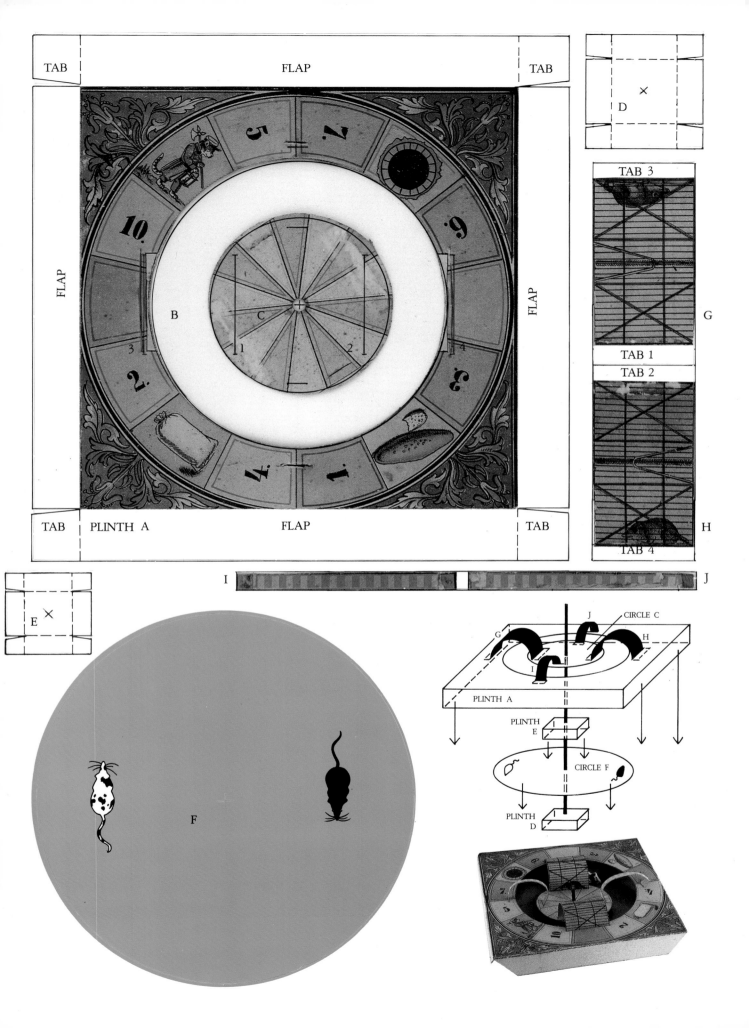

TAB

FLAP

TAB

D

TAB 3

FLAP

5

7

10

9

FLAP

B

C

1

2

G

2

3

TAB 1

TAB 2

4

1

TAB

PLINTH A

FLAP

TAB

H

TAB 4

I

J

E

J

CIRCLE C

G

H

I

PLINTH A

PLINTH
E

CIRCLE F

F

PLINTH
D

Cat on a Pole

HOW TO ASSEMBLE

1 Push out Cat's head, body and legs. Take a pin or folded staple and join the head to the body at point A. Check that the head moves freely; join the front legs at either side of the body at point B and do likewise with the back legs at point C. The legs should move freely. Put Cat to one side.

2 Push out sections F and G. Take F and fold it along the marked lines to make a thin square stick. Glue the strips marked 'flap' together. Repeat with section G. You now have two sticks – one short, one long.

3 Push out section H. Push out the holes marked '1' and '2'. Fold H down the middle and glue together. Push out the two tabs marked I, fold them into right-angles (like the letter L). Glue these tabs either side of hole marked '1'.

4 Take stick F, put it into hole '1' and, leaving two inches of stick hanging out of the bottom, glue the stick firmly in place using the tabs. Take stick G, the long one, and put it into hole '2'. Do not glue: this stick must move freely up and down.

5 Take the Cat, pin his front paws either side of the top of stick F. Fix Cat's back paws either side of the top of stick G.

6 Check your model with the illustration and take the stick F in your hand and with your other hand push and pull stick G up and down to make Cat perform. Clever acrobat, lissomly charismatic.

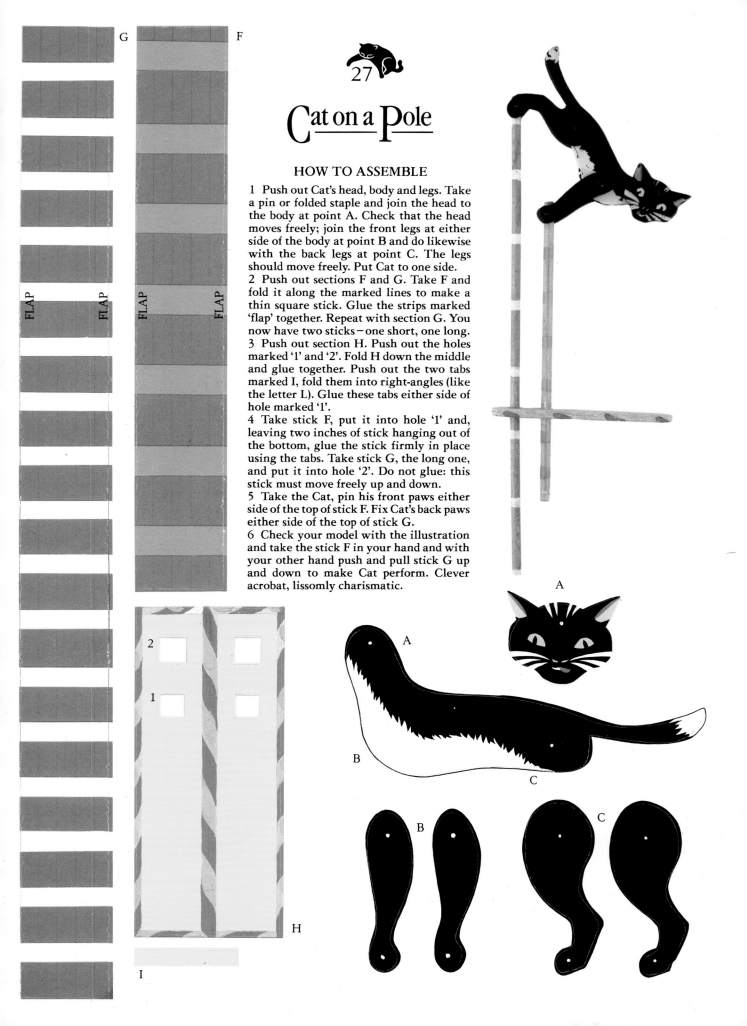

G

F

FLAP

FLAP

FLAP

FLAP

2

1

H

I

A

A

B

C

B

C

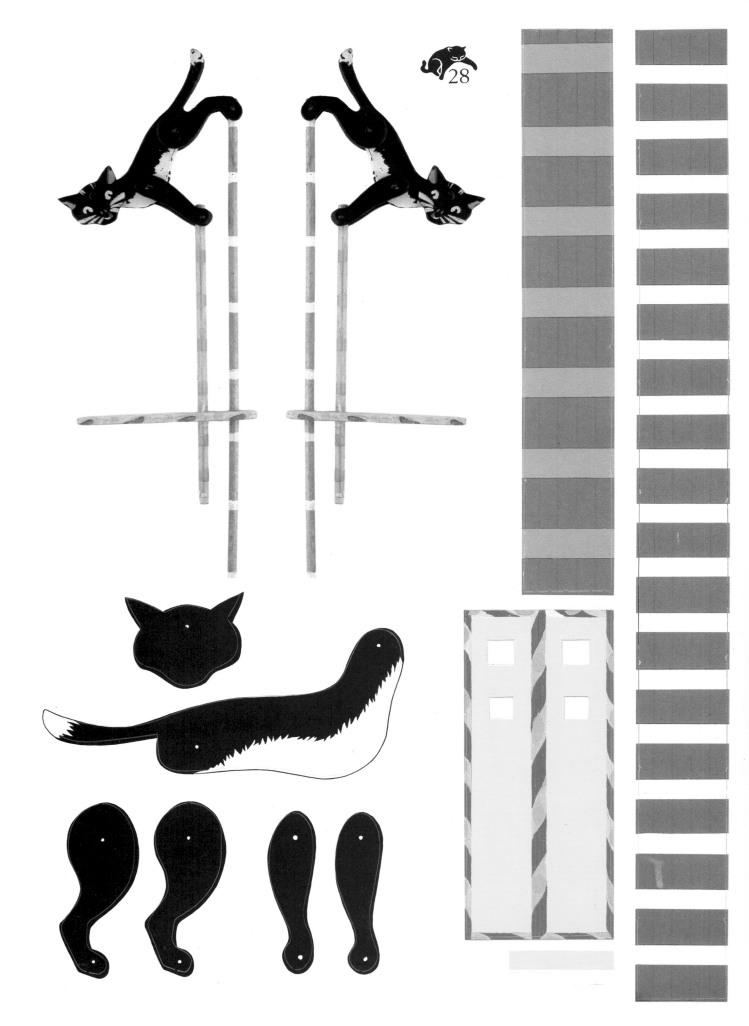

The Little Kittens

HOW TO PLAY

You need several sets of counters in different colours: you can press out the counters on page 33, but for this game plastic 'tiddly-wink' counters are better.

As many players can play as there are different colours of counters. Put the little kittens upright on a table; the players sit together in front of the little kittens. Each player has one large counter – the *flipper* – as well as a set of small ones. The aim is to flip your counters into the mouths of the kittens using the flipper. The number of points you get each time depends on which paw your counter falls through. The player with the highest number of points WINS.

TAB

FLAP 3

FLAP 1

HOW TO ASSEMBLE

1 Push out the Cats, their mouths, and their circles at 2, 4, 1, 5.

2 Push out the section marked 'box'. Fold up the flaps 1, 2 and 3 towards you into right angles. Use the tabs to glue them into the box shape.

3 Fold flap 4 up and flat against the inside of the box, glue it firmly. Fold flap 6 towards you into a right angle. You should use this flap to glue the box to the back of the cats. Use tape round the box to make the assembly secure. If you look up the Cats' paws you should see that the ramp inside is sloping down towards you.

FLAP 4

FLAP 6

FLAP 2

BOX

TAB

Howling Cat

HOW TO ASSEMBLE

1 Push out the Cat's head and body, his four legs and his tail.
2 Using pins, thin wire, or folded staples fix the Cat's front legs at point A; the back legs at B, and the tail...?

HOW TO PLAY

Each player takes a turn in wearing a blindfold. The Cat is pinned on the wall, the blindfolded player is given the Cat's tail and must try to pin the tail as near to point C as possible. The person who gets the tail nearest to the right place WINS.

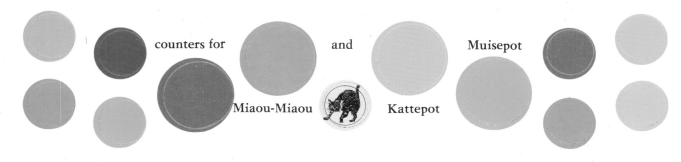

counters for **Miaou-Miaou** and **Kattepot** **Muisepot**

Counters and Finger Puppets

HOW TO ASSEMBLE
1 Press out the finger puppets.
2 Press out the strips and bend and glue each strip into a ring.

3 Glue each Cat to a ring and you end up with six finger puppets.
Press out the counters as and when you need them for the board games.

rats and cats for La Pontica and Kilkenny Cats

rats and cats for La Pontica and Kilkenny Cats

white cats for La Pontica and Kilkenny Cats

rats and cats for La Pontica and Kilkenny Cats

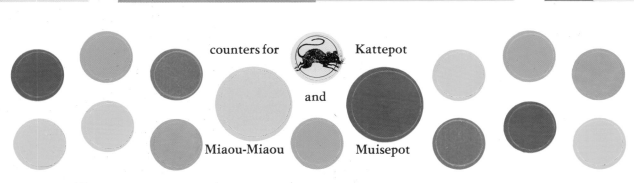

counters for **Kattepot** and **Miaou-Miaou** **Muisepot**

♠ The Past

♥ The Present

♣ The Past

♦ The Present

BLACK CAT
Fortune Telling Cards

♠ The Present

♥ The Past

♣ The Present

♦ The Past

1 You have had an eventful past; you have
1 Your temper has caused you much
1 Your quarreling disposition has deprived
1 You have been in the habit of not telling
1 Your flirtations, although of an innocent
1 Your indiscretions in the past have harmed
2 Your rivals an opportunity to misrepresent
2 Have been torturing yourself with jealousy
3 Are treated to a dose of the same medicine
4 To keep your poor children from starvation.
3 Always enjoyed a good reputation, but
4 Supposed you were the hero of the hour.
2 Is because you have entertained such
2 Wishes and many, many tears have you
3 And so effectively that even your enemies
4 And possess as many admirers as you do.
4 Are only paying you back in your own coin.
3 But much of your trouble could have
2 Trouble in the past, and your suspicious
2 In the past, your heart has been subjected
3 Has estranged the love and affections of many
4 But it is too late to atone the wrong.
4 Tormenting those who know how to enjoy life.
3 Prevented many mistakes, which

2 By your personal beauty, but your stupidity
4 Surprise that will paralyze you.
2 In looks, and defective in form, but you
3 Faith and with sincere intentions it will
3 But you will have very poor success
4 Opposed by the folks on both sides.
1 Expect a letter full of good news
1 You have at present something on your
1 Something unpleasant is preparing
1 You have made a hasty promise which
1 You are now having a grand time by talking
1 The object of your first love is being
4 A wrong opinion of you.
3 Style. Your smooth talk and good manners
2 For you much admiration, but your
2 So much in the days of your youth
3 You will meet with good success and
4 By ignoring the party.
4 Him and he will molest you no more.
3 Faultless, but in a few years you will be
2 You would like to own as your friends
2 Ambition is to be pretty; your thoughts are
3 Old and true friends, but bear in mind
4 Some of your handsome and boastful friends.

4 Your future will be still more eventful.
3 In repenting your rash acts and foolish
3 Of bursting into tears on slight provocations
2 The truth, and this is one of the principal
4 Is very near you.
2 Your good name and reputation, but your
4 Established at the expense of your enemies.
3 For which there really was no cause as you
4 You are vexed and play the baby act.
3 Need it very much in the near future
2 Had your share of good and bad luck. You
2 To be flattered, and often you have been
3 A high estimation of yourself that
4 Enjoying themselves to their heart's content.
4 Admire you for your pluck.
3 Few people who have so many true friends
2 Have lost you many a true friend, whom you
2 Met with troubles and disappointments
1 Your jealous disposition has caused you much
1 You have had quite a few disappointments
1 Your sensitive disposition has caused
1 Your trifling with the feelings of those
1 If in the past you had thought more of your
1 If you had not been born so smart, you would

1 You are at present eliciting much admiration
1 Your flirtations are at present a source of
1 You are not at fault that you are homely
1 There is a person who has made you a promise
1 Your expectations are about to realize;
1 Prepare for a very sudden acquaintance
2 Which will make you decide to take
2 Mind, which causes you much worry
3 You will triumph, and will win the
4 Consequence will be trouble and disappointment.
3 Few years it may be necessary to take in
4 One of your journeys.
2 With your left eye, and that fact has
2 Your dress; you disarm criticism in get-up and
3 Ignorance and stupidity are universal
4 Made a rash choice and will be happy.
4 Become very wealthy and receive high honors.
3 But you are now trying to play even
2 Man, whom you have shown many favors
2 The styles, and your style and appearance is
3 But your proud disposition will not permit
4 And dearest wish is to be wealthy
4 You will regret it, and repent when too late.
3 And raise a family of prettier children than

4 Of much comment and are universally detested.
3 And you may prepare for a genuine
3 Make matters still worse by your persistent
2 But, although the promise was made in good
4 With your new undertaking.
2 With a blue-eyed and dark complexioned
4 You to receive a large sum of money.
3 The sooner you will act according to dictates
4 Admiration of one you love very much.
3 Circumstances compel you to do so, and the
2 In balls, receptions and sociables, but in a
2 Married this very hour. You will meet
3 Led one very near to you to form
4 Are bewitching, but your face is homely.
4 Regretted and deplored.
3 Is being married to-day. He has, however
2 Signifies that after much trouble and hardships
2 Who has offended you and refuses to apologize
1 You are being annoyed by a young
1 It keeps you very busy now to keep up with
1 Your stubbornness is offending many whom
1 Your religion is to be in style; your highest
1 Your new friend has succeeded with flattery
1 Nature has not endowed you with physical

2 Borne troubles with admirable fortitude
4 Capers while laboring under such spells.
2 You of many opportunities and your habits
3 Reasons why a party who once
3 You in the estimation of one who
4 The battle boldly and you will succeed better.
1 Your lively disposition in the past has given
1 You have led a life of misery because you
1 It has been your delight to trifle with
1 You have been spending your money too
1 You have wept, you have laughed, you have
1 Your weakness has been that you enjoyed
4 You hardly knew that other people existed.
3 Shed in quiet solitude, while others were
2 But you have borne them heroically
2 Eventful past than you, but there are very
3 Now accused of being unfaithful, while they
4 Been prevented had you been less stubborn.
4 Loved and adored you.
3 To many severe tests, but you are
2 You much trouble and annoyance and
2 Who will not recognize your dictations has
3 Now be on earth for the sole purpose of
4 Are now the source of much regret to you.

3 Ignorance and ill-manners are the cause
2 Much pleasure to you, but you are watched
4 Habit of chewing gum and greasing your hair.
4 Not be kept on account of a misunderstanding.
2 Your fondest hopes will soon be fulfilled,
3 Person, which will be vigorously
3 A journey, and which will occasion
4 Of your own conscience the better it will be.
2 For you, if you will meet it boldly,
2 You never intend to keep or fulfill, but
4 Washing to keep starvation from your door.
3 The couple very unexpectedly on
1 You have acquired a habit of winking
1 You are exhibiting much taste in
1 Your beauty and good form are winning
1 The young man with whom you chummed
1 You have a mole on your back which
1 You are troubling your mind about a person
3 But his failure to worry you has discouraged
4 Hustling to keep your family from starvation.
4 You to offer an apology.
3 Spend in self admiration and your fondest
2 And polished talk to turn you against your
2 Beauty, but for all that you may be happier

3 But unless you change your conduct
2 Trouble, and many a tear have you shed
4 Has disgusted many who once admired you.
4 Admired you is now avoiding you.
2 Character, have resulted in lowering
3 Lamentations only make matters worse. Face
3 Your character, but your innocence will be
4 Actually never had any rivals.
2 Other people's feelings, but now when you
2 Freely, stop and save some of it as you will
4 Your conduct of late arouses suspicion.
3 Made the target of fun while you
1 The reason why you have so few friends
1 Fate has disappointed many of your fondest
1 You have had your share of trouble
1 There are many people who have had a more
1 Your independent ways and vain disposition
1 You have had many ups and downs, you have
3 Ways have angered many who once
4 All right now, and look in a bright future.
4 Who once were dear friends to you.
3 Estranged you one whom you now admire
2 God, and less of yourself, you would not
2 Have heeded the advice of your parents, and

♣ The Future

♦ Love Matters

♠ The Future

♠ Love Matters

The great games firm of Parker Brothers issued *The Black Cat Fortune Telling Game* in 1897. It was, and is, a game 'for all seasons but highly recommended for Halloween'. You can practise this game by laying out the cards and reading your own fortune – you don't even need another player.

The pack of fortune-telling cards consists of six sets of four cards each – the Past, the Present, the Future, Love Matters, General Advice, and Danger – twenty-four cards in all. On the back of each card is all the information you need to tell your fortune, arranged in twenty-four lines. Each line is numbered and you

♥ Love Matters

♥ The Future

♣ Love Matters

♦ The Future

4 Circumstances will prevent you from doing so.
3 The girls will become confirmed old maids
3 To desist from taking the important step, but
2 Announcing the death of a relative for whom
4 Experience much sickness in your own family.
2 You will experience sudden prosperity, and
4 In making a large fortune.
3 You a large legacy, but it will be contested
4 Will live to a very old age.
3 But she will grow up to a lovely woman, and
2 To visit one of your friends but before
2 Which you could have prevented
3 Have many children, mostly boys, who will
4 Will return disgusted with traveling.
4 Make you enemies who envy your good luck.
3 Person is married you will receive such marked
2 That will give you great prominence. But
2 An event in which you will be the center
1 You will have your hardships and will fight
1 You will go to a distant country where your
1 Your fondest wish will be fulfilled in the near
1 Prepare for a genuine sensation in your family
1 You will meet an old acquaintance, whom you
1 You will experience unfaithfulness in love, and

2 Rich, but a smiling face, a devoted heart and
3 With a pair of handsome twins, but sickness
4 Terror to your surroundings.
4 Know the art of how to love.
3 Love you possess will make it an object to
2 Dwell in mansions, but you will be happy in the
1 The one you love is not rich in money, but
1 Do not believe for a moment that you possess
1 The love which you spend so freely on your
1 Your love is wasted on some one who is
1 The love that is being bestowed upon you is
1 After you have spent eleven happy years in
4 That will bring you much joy and happiness.
3 Deprived you of everything you will wed
4 Another, death will suddenly end your career.
3 Who will love you tenderly and one who is
2 Make it an object to cultivate this love it will
2 Some heart to vibrate, which will arouse a love
1 Not realize it or you would make an effort
4 You really love is loving some one else.
2 Married life in happiness, and will be blessed
2 The love which will be bestowed upon
3 Part of your married life, but mutual love
4 Happy and will die with a broken heart.

1 You will receive a letter from an unexpected
1 You will raise a family of eleven children
1 Your parents will oppose your prospective
1 You will receive a letter of importance
1 You will suffer the loss of one of your
1 You will be favored with very good luck
2 To a red-haired person, whom you will at
2 But little, will die within a year, and leave
3 Suffer much with sickness, but you
4 Will be the pride of the family.
3 You return something will transpire that
4 Of following the dictates of a deceitful person.
2 And will accumulate riches. You will also
3 You to undertake a journey, but you will meet
3 It will make you very popular, but it will also
3 Attention that it will arouse jealousy.
4 Glory will soon give way to sad disappointment.
3 Of attraction, but it will also signify the
2 Many battles against ill fate, but you will be
2 Will meet with great success in all of your
3 Circumstances that will convert your joy,
4 Much annoyance and humiliation.
4 Much jealousy that will result in trouble.
3 Intimate friend has been false to you and has

1 The one you love is neither handsome nor
1 Your wedded partner will be true to you. You
1 You are too whimsical and deceitful to
1 You enjoy being loved; it affords you
1 You are one of the very few whose love
1 You perhaps never will possess riches nor
4 Be, because you are a confirmed crank.
3 One you love as a great deal of it is lavished
3 Would not treat you to love that is being
4 Rejected over a dozen times.
2 Sincere and affectionate, and originates in a
2 Married life, your wedded partner will elope
3 Will lead to a separation and end in a marriage
4 The one whose faithful love you once rejected.
2 Twice you will be married and twice you will
2 An agreeable and generous temper, one
4 Will land you in the sea of eternal happiness.
3 That will lull you to dreaming in the arms
4 Fan the spark of love to its former brilliancy.
3 The best of your ability, but the one whom
4 Bring you and your family to grief.
3 You will be sincere and tender and
2 Quarrels and disputes in the early
2 You will travel and see all the wonders of the

will find that when the cards have been arranged according to the rules, on only one of the lines do the numbers 1, 2, 3 and 4 read consecutively across the row from left to right. That is the line that you must read to divine your fortune. Push out each card from the page and you are ready.

HOW TO PLAY

1 Shuffle the pack of cards thoroughly. Hand them, picture side up, to the person whose fortune you are telling so that he or she can cut them and place them on the table between you, still picture side up. You should then take one card at a time from the

4 In married life than wealth or beauty.
4 Will deprive you of much happiness.
3 Quarrelsome disposition make you a
2 Much pleasure to be embraced. You
2 Path will be strewn with roses. The one whose
3 Embrace of one whose true and affectionate
3 Will not be a paradise on earth it will
4 On a handsome, but depraved person.
2 Beloved one is not appreciated, or else the party
2 Not worthy of it. While your love is honest
3 Heart that is both true and noble, and that
4 Broken-hearted to the mercy of your enemies.
2 Love of one whom you do not love. A scandal
2 A sudden termination. But after death has
3 Be divorced, although you frantically love
4 Only happy when your happiness is complete.
4 Grow more passionate until finally it
4 Of unadulterated bliss and happiness.
1 The flame of love which gladdened your heart
1 It is true that you are being loved, and it is
1 You will spend the first few years of your
1 The one you love is honest and industrious and
1 Your stubbornness will lead to many
1 You will be very prosperous in married life

3 Which you would like to accept, but
2 Six of these will be girls, and five will be boys.
4 If you will be firm all will end well.
4 Made you the sole heir of a large fortune.
2 Nearest relatives by death, and will sustain
3 Enjoy great respect from high personages, but
3 First despise, but who will assist you
4 By relatives, and a lawsuit will be the result.
2 Of your family by death, and you will
2 Trouble and dissention in married life
4 Will prove a genuine surprise to you.
3 Had you consulted your friends, instead
1 You will be successful in life and in love
1 Your restless disposition will cause
1 In the near future you will engage in a new
1 You will meet a highly respected person who
1 You will meet with circumstances
1 Before another year lapses, you will celebrate
3 Successful in all and will rise to unexpected
4 Land after you have become very wealthy.
4 And happiness into bitter disappointment.
3 Not directly concern you, but will cause you
2 Have not seen for many years, although it
2 Will learn to your greatest surprise that your

3 Loving disposition is far more essential
2 Will have a comfortable home and be blessed
2 Cultivate love. Your ill temper and
3 Never tire of being kissed, but you do not
4 Make you the happiest being on earth.
4 Heart will bring you more joy than wealth.
2 Rich in love, and if your married life
2 The full and undivided affections of the
4 Lavished on others of a questionable character.
3 And true, you are treated to love that has been
4 Beats for nothing but your happiness.
3 With a near relative of yours, and leave you
1 You will start out in married life guarded by the
1 Your married life, though happy will have
1 Your married life will be romantic.
1 The one you love is a person who possesses
1 You are loved and much loved, and if you will
1 Your sighs for love has set the strings of
2 Is dying out, and what is worse you do
2 Equally true that you are returning the love to
3 With lovely children, but dissipation will
4 Your home will be a veritable paradise.
4 Will triumph and lead you to happiness.
3 World, but you will never be loved nor be made

2 Source, containing a very flattering proposal
4 While the boys will be notorious as cranks.
2 Undertaking, and will try to persuade you
3 You have never had great respect, but who has
3 A loss of money; besides you will
4 A letter will bring you very sad news.
1 You will get an unexpected introduction
1 An uncle of whom you know and have heard
1 You will mourn the loss of several members
1 A child with red hair will cause you much
1 You will soon undertake a long journey
1 You will meet with great trouble
4 Be the source of much trouble to you.
3 With so many unpleasant adventures, that you
2 Enterprise that will meet with success
2 Holds a prominent position. Although the
3 Your conduct will be so awkward that your
4 Beginning with a life of trouble for you.
4 Dignity, and will grow very wealthy.
3 Undertakings, and will return to your native
2 Future, but you will be confronted with
2 That will attract universal attention. It will
2 Will afford you much pleasure, it will lead to
4 The affections of one whom you love so dearly.

♣ General Advice

♥ DANGER!

♠ General Advice

♠ DANGER!

top of the pack, and, without looking at the lines on the back, arrange them (words down) from left to right in six rows in the following order: the Past; the Present; the Future; Love Matters; General Advice; Danger.

2 When all the cards have been arranged you can reveal the fortune you are seeking. Turn over the cards in the first row and find the line in which the numbers 1, 2, 3 and 4 run consecutively from left to right: these will disclose the past. Do the same with the second row of cards to discover the present and on to the future and all the rest.

♦ DANGER!

♦ General Advice

♣ DANGER!

♥ General Advice

1 Do not worry your head about that dark
1 Never ridicule or poke fun at people
1 Do not despair.   Be hopeful and remember
1 If you will do less talking and more thinking
1 Never sing or play while you are in company
1 Face danger bravely; fight the battles
4 Those whom you have so grossly offended.
3 Or else you will sacrifice the love of
3 For which you have been wishing so
4 Change, while there is snow on the ground.
2 Luck; therefore be industrious, and that will
2 And greasing your hair, you will
3 Friends.   Try and reconcile him, you will need
4 You the appearance of a second-hand wax doll.
2 Better, if you stop worrying over every little
2 Triumph over your enemies, who are now
4 Or you will never be happy.
3 Will gain friends and win the respect of a
4 And you will need their assistance.
3 Those who confide in you, and many think
4 A prominent position in public life.
3 Pay more attention to those who try to
2 Of appreciation is enough to make a saint swear
2 Which, if cultivated will lead you to great

4 You real happy, therefore beware!
4 A dangerous person who seeks your ruin.
3 Deceive you.   Take him to task at once, or he
2 Decline them.   Do not commit yourself in
2 Will not be granted.   Be more modest in
3 And act politely, but if you are not on your
3 Her personal beauty, but who is laying
4 Days which will always result in success.
2 If ever so little insist upon a speedy
2 Enemies, who will try to do you an
3 Talk.   Be on your guard and show no
4 Traveling by water for at least six months.
2 For the purpose of deceiving you.   Keep a close
2 Misrepresented to you.   It is a clever scheme
3 Unless you act more agreeably, you
4 Have the effect of harming your good name.
3 Place no credence in what he says
4 And treat them with utmost suspicion.
1 You will contract a severe illness by exposure,
1 While taking a drive your horse will become
1 You will have a quarrel with your neighbor
1 When you are traveling, select a room in the
1 You will meet a gentleman, who will make
1 You will receive an insulting letter from an

3 Never be carried out, therefore ignore him
2 Who have red hair, because one of your
2 That you are young and have a life time
3 Your company would be more agreeable
4 You were in ———— heaven.
4 In possession of a large fortune.
2 Changes in your conduct you may regain.
2 Don't show your fondness for dancing
4 Long will soon transpire.
3 Meet with good luck.   But do not make the
4 It will bring you wealth.
3 Become a favorite in society and an
1 You have made a deplorable mistake in
1 Your complexion would be much improved
1 You will be happier and will enjoy life
1 Be honest and industrious and you will
1 Be more sincere in your love, and do not
1 If you will be more benevolent to the poor
2 Good business education, because the time will
2 You have been in the habit of deceiving
3 With such qualifications that are essential in
4 Make you happy or else you will come to grief.
4 Agreeable, or you will land in the mad house.
3 Prosperity, and besides will have a tendency to

1 If you will not stop flirting it will deprive
1 Before the moon changes again you will
1 Your most intimate friend, to whom you have
1 Whatever your intentions are, for the present
1 If your desires are too extravagant they
1 Fear a man with a black moustache and
4 A plot to ruin your happiness.
3 The 7th and 17th are your lucky.
3 Settlement and expect a letter
4 Friend in whom you confided so much of late.
2 Deceived by flattery and polished
2 You must be very careful or else you will meet
3 Watch and avoid a person who will endeavor to
4 Prove to be the grandest mistake of your life.
2 Subject of much comment among your friends
2 Reflect very seriously upon your character
2 Because his motives are prompted by malice.
3 House.   Keep your eyes on beggars and tramps
4 May terminate in sudden death.
3 Remain in the carriage and do not jump
4 Will commit a crime that will land you in prison.
3 Stand great risk of being burned to death, also
2 It a point to insult you.   Do not enter in any
2 Unknown source.   Do not accuse an enemy of

2 You of the love and esteem of one who loves
3 Do not cultivate his friendship as he is
4 Will succeed in destroying your good name.
4 And your expectations will realize.
3 Your demands and more economical in
2 Piercing black eyes.   He will talk friendly
1 Be on your guard for an ill-bred and
1 Never undertake anything on the 13th day
1 Look well to those who owe you money
1 You have at present a number of secret
1 You have a dangerous rival.   Be not
1 You have reached a stage in your life, where
4 Attract your attention by a generous offer.
3 To deceive you, and if successful it would
4 Will never rise above your present condition.
3 Make an effort to check this talk or it will
2 Trouble between you and one of your relatives
2 An attempt will be made to burglarize your
3 And exercise the greatest care, your sickness
4 As that would mean sure death.
2 That will result in a lawsuit.   Keep control
2 Hotel that has a fire escape or else you
3 Disputes, because he is a desperate character,
4 A near relative of yours is the guilty person.

4 And he will disappear and never molest you.
4 Which though red will be much admired.
3 Before you, and that you will have your share
2 And will stop your everlasting quarreling
2 Or when your neighbors are at home as it may
3 Be rewarded, and very unexpectedly come
3 That which you have lost and reconcile
4 One who loves you most sincerely.
2 Dignified and independent, the happy result
2 Locate in a northerly direction, you will
3 Bring you sure gain, and if you persevere
4 Object of much admiration.
2 Slighting and offending one of your truest
2 If you would wash your face with water instead
3 Mishap, which only has a tendency to make life
4 Enterprise that would ruin you.
3 Be less deceitful and more appreciative
4 Community, who now denounce and despise you.
1 Be kind to your children, and give them a
1 Be more frank and upright to your friends
1 Devote more time to reading, show a more
1 Your melancholical and inactive disposition
1 Your indolent and peevish temper with no sense
1 You are naturally gifted and possess talent

3 You sincerely, and who is in a position to make
2 Receive an introduction to a tall gentleman
2 Confided so much of late, is planning to
3 Anyway as those who are absent will return
4 Your dress or else you will come to grief.
4 Guard, he will effect your ruin.
2 Scandal loving woman, who is noted for
2 Of any month, as it will bring you bad luck
4 In which your life is threatened.
3 Injury.   Be on your guard and watch an intimate
4 Weakness or else you will be trapped.
3 With fatal accidents.   Above all things avoid
1 A treacherous person is seeking your friendship
1 Hold fast to a friend who will be grossly
1 Your thoughtless disposition has been the
1 Your enemies have started a rumor, that
1 A young gentleman, will try to create
1 Lock your doors and windows at night, because
2 And unless you will consult a physician at once
2 Unmanageable, and will indulge in a runaway
3 Of your temper and do not get excited or you
4 Avoid traveling on the 13th day of any month.
4 And is capable of doing you great bodily harm.
3 Being the author of the letter, because

2 Complexioned man.   His threats will
3 Children will have a beautiful head of red locks
4 Of this world's blessings, if you only persevere.
4 To those with whom you associate.
3 Have a tendency to make them wish
2 Of life courageously, and some day you will
1 If you will apologize and will make radical
1 Don't be too forward, don't chew gum
1 If you will become less anxious, and more
1 If you will change your residence, and
1 You will never thrive by what is called good
1 If you will quit chewing gum, eating onions
4 Him to shape your future happiness.
3 Of greasing it with beauty paste, which gives
4 A burden to you and to your surroundings.
3 Doing their utmost to interest you in an
2 Pay any attention to outward appearance.
2 And be more kind to your surroundings, you
3 Come when poverty will stare you in the face
4 You are acting the part of a hypocrite.
2 Industrious disposition, and equip yourself
2 Is disgusting one who once admired you.
3 Change your conduct and act more
4 Make you a universal favorite in society.

BOARD GAMES

There exists a certain, though understandable belief that cats are extremely solitary animals and it is true that they display independence, a certain *sang froid* when in the company of other cats. But nevertheless there is also an abundance of evidence to suggest that cats are indeed capable of making friends among their own kind. They have been seen rubbing heads together or settling down together for a mutually comfortable catatonic trance or deep sleep. However, they do not, it seems, unless they have been very discreet about the activity, indulge in board games. Only humans and the occasional, frighteningly precocious monkey play board games. Cats are missing out on an entire world of friendly rivalry and convivial competition. Have fun.

A cat's end game in draughts can be finished off with feline finesse in a duel, whereas pretty kittens prefer to play and patter. However kittens grow up.

Miau! Miau!

Miau! Miau!

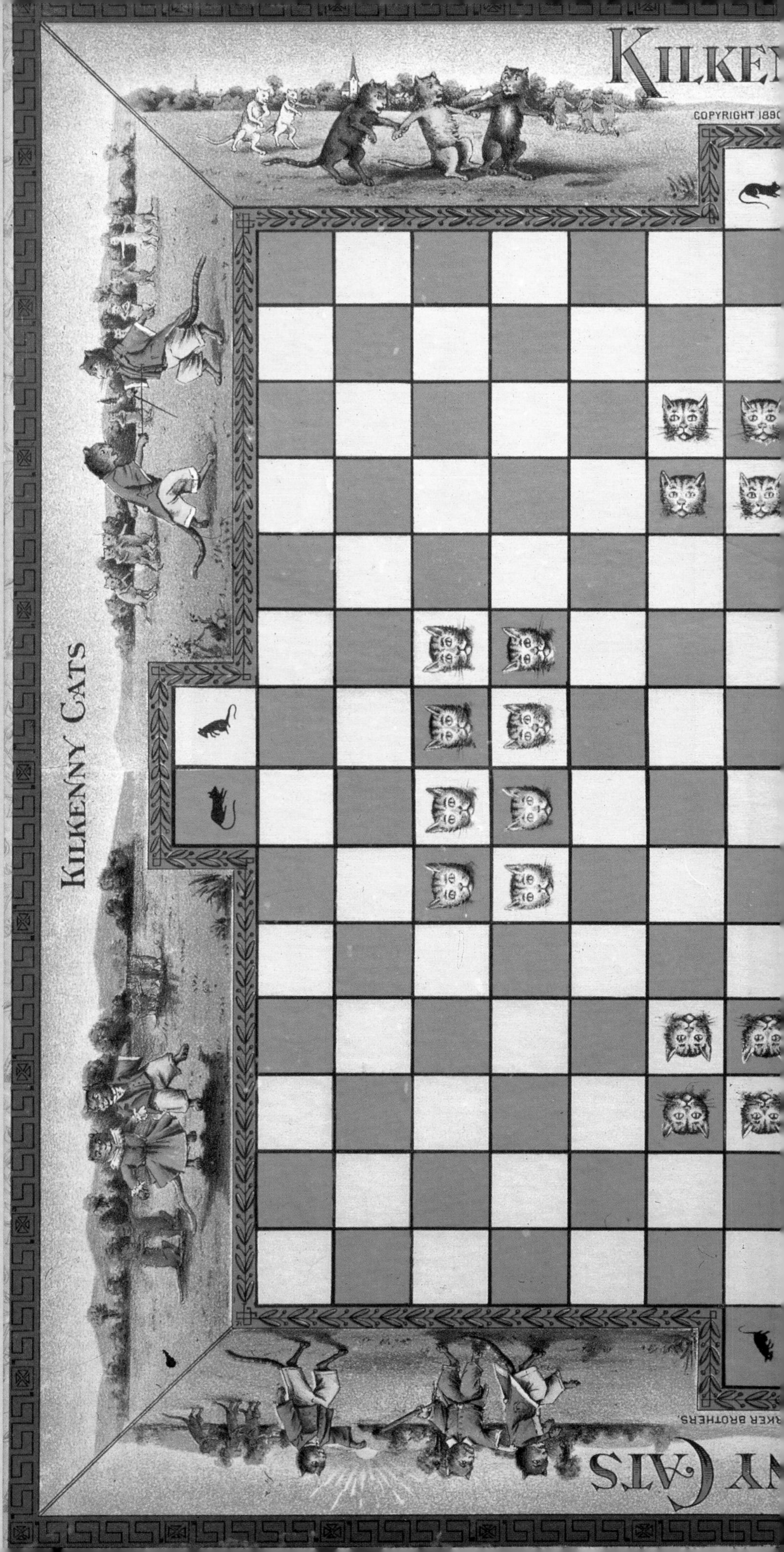
KILKENNY CATS

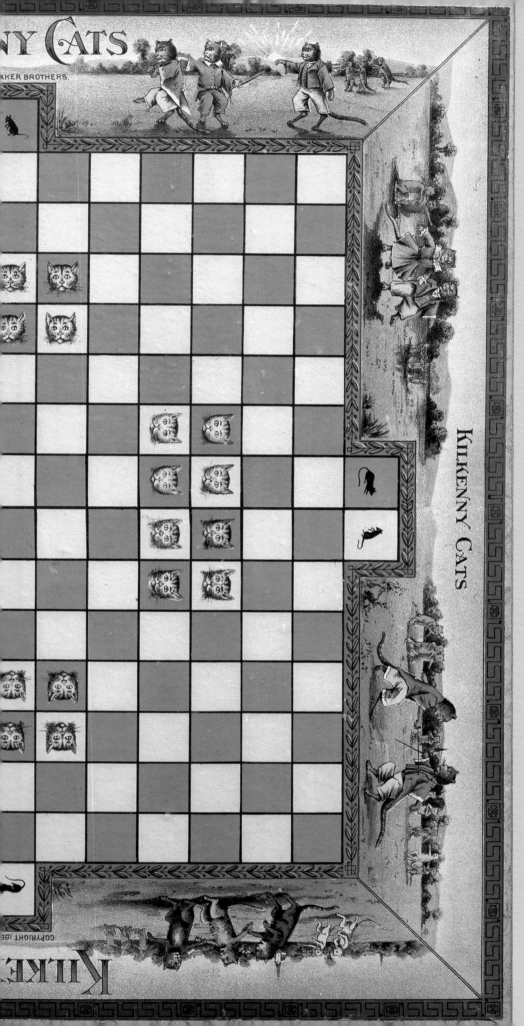

45

Courtesy:
The Washington Dolls' House
and Toy Museum

46

KATTEPOT

Uitlegging hoe ...

1. Men speelt dit spiksplinternieuwe spel maar met twee personen. De een is **kat** en de ander is **muis**. Men heeft slechts twee gewone dobbelsteenen noodig.

2. De inzet, die de **kat** en de **muis** ieder in haar eigen pot brengen, is onbepaald. De **kat** begint links van boven en telt naar den **muizepot**. De **muis** begint rechts van onder en telt naar den **kattepot**. Om de nummers te bezetten, heeft ieder een afzonderlijk voorwerp.

3. De **roode** nummers maken den **katteweg** en de **zwarte** den **muizeweg**.

4. Men werpt wie het eerst begint en deze is de **kat**.

4. Wie bij den eersten worp [·][·] gooit komt op 11, wie op of over 11 is en [·][·] gooit komt op 22. — Wie op of over 22 is en [∴][∴] gooit komt op 33. — Wie op of over

33 is en [⊞][⊞] gooit, komt op 44. — Wie op of over 55 is en [⊞][⊞] gooit, k alles wat er in staat, haalt zijn eigen po

6. Komt de **kat** op 11, 22, 33, 44 en

7. Komt de **muis** op 11, 22, 33, 44 en

8. Wie [⊞][⊞] gooit voor hij op of over speler en blijft staan waar hij staat. Wie penningen aan zijnen medespeler betalen en lijke nummers tellen op de gewone wijze

UITGAVE van J. VLIEGER, AMSTERDAM.

MUIZEPOT

47

lit spel spelen moet.

over 44 is en ⊞ ⊞ gooit, komt op 55, en
den pot van zijnen medespeler en neemt
it en het spel is uit.

n krijgt ze twee penningen van de **muis**.
an krijgt ze twee penningen van de **kat**.
betaalt twee penningen aan zijnen mede-
ersten worp reeds ⊞ ⊞ gooit, moet twee
van den inzet bij zijn eigen pot. Andere ge-
e in de gevallen in artikel 4 genoemd.

9. Wanneer de **kat** springt over een nummer, dat door de **muis** bezet is, dan betaalt
zij een penning aan de **muis**. Springt de **muis** over een nummer, dat door de **kat** bezet is,
dan betaalt zij een penning aan de **kat**. Bijvoorbeeld. De **muis** staat op 39 en de **kat** moet
van 24 naar 28, dan zal hij over 39 moeten springen.

10. Wie op 55 of daarboven staat en een getal werpt, dat over de 66 komt, gaat terug naar 48.

11. Worden er geene gelijke cijfers geworpen, dan wordt de pot gewonnen op de gewone wijze.

12. Wie op 5, 15, 25, 35, 45 of 65 komt moet zijne beurt eenmaal laten voorbijgaan.

13. Wie op 10, 20, 30, 40, 50 of 60 komt mag nog eens werpen.

14. Wie op 4, 9, 16, 25, 49 of 64 komt betaalt een penning aan zijnen medespeler.   P. L.

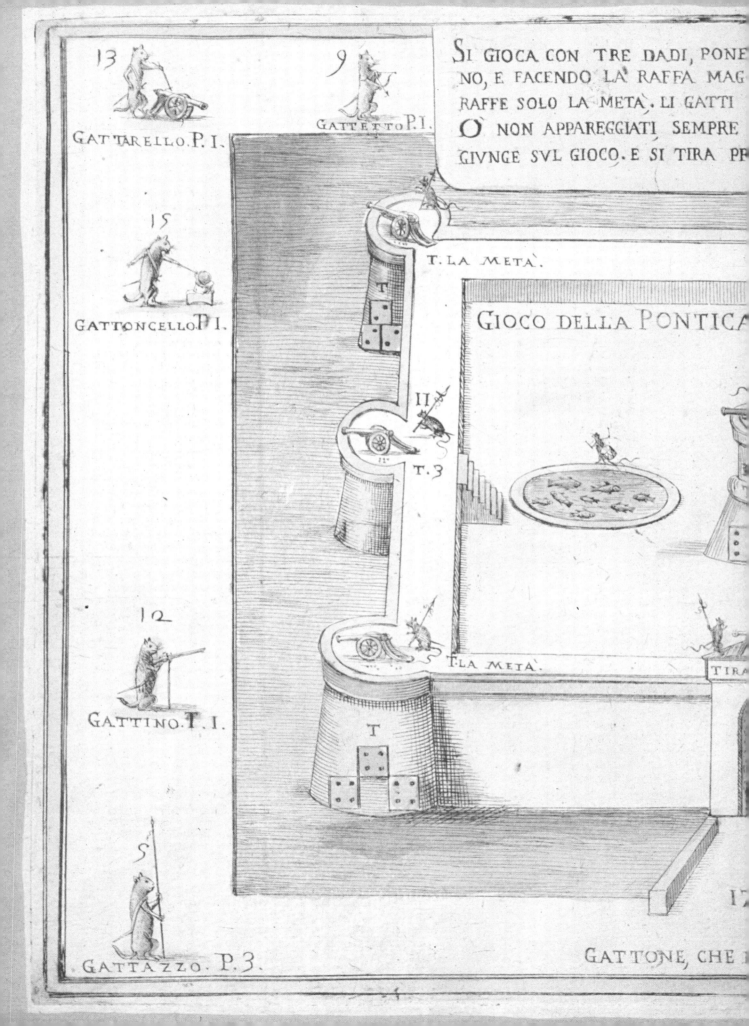

13

GATTARELLO. P. I.

9

GATTETTO P. I.

15

GATTONCELLO P. I.

T. LA METÀ.

T

GIOCO DELLA PONTICA

II

T. 3

12

GATTINO. T. I.

T. LA METÀ.

T

S

GATTAZZO. P. 3.

TIRA

GATTONE, CHE

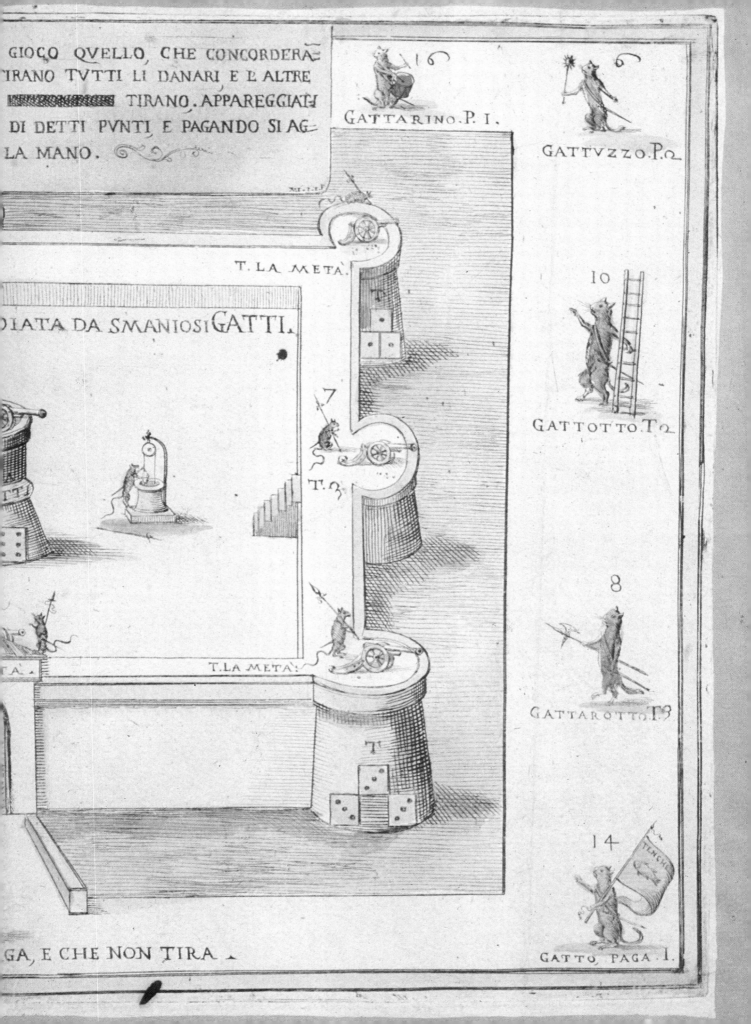

GIOCO QVELLO, CHE CONCORDERAŘ
TIRANO TVTTI LI DANARI E L'ALTRE
████████████ TIRANO. APPAREGGIATI
DI DETTI PVNTI, E PAGANDO SI AG-
LA MANO.

GATTARINO. P. I.

GATTVZZO. P. 2

...DIATA DA SMANIOSI GATTI.

T. LA METÀ.

10

GATTOTTO. T. 2

7

T. 3

8

GATTAROTTO. T. 3

T. LA METÀ.

14

...GA, E CHE NON TIRA.

GATTO. PAGA. I.

Sister Catkins

Sister Catkins is a feline variation on an American game, known as *Brother Jonathan,* which was already old in 1881. Any number can play and all that is needed is a small but fairly heavy coin – and skill.

RULES OF PLAY

1 Lay the book open on a table and choose a mark from which to pitch your coin; the distance will depend on the age and height of the players and can be extended as you grow more skilled.

2 Taking turns, pitch the coin at the cats' heads. As you can see, the smaller the cats' heads, the greater the score.

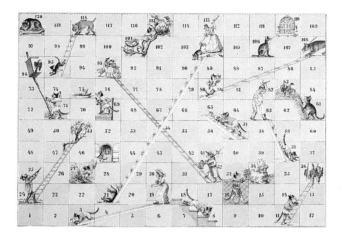

Miaou! Miaou!

'The great success of our *Circus Game and Game of Frogs* has led us this year to present a most original and amusing game of cats and ladders called *Miaou! Miaou!* We hope our game will attract scores of friends,' wrote the anonymous French publisher (box cover, games sheet and rules give no clue to his identity) of *Miaou! Miaou!* It was probably published around 1905; the decades either side of 1900 seem to have been a fertile time for cat game inventors.

The game of *Miaou! Miaou!* is about the adventures of the tomcat Ronron, on whose colourful chequered board we are shown the manoeuvres he follows to reach his favourite place on a cushion at the fireside.

RULES OF PLAY

1 This is a game for two to six players and requires two dice and six tokens. Each player chooses a token and takes his turn to throw one of the dice; he then places his token on the square whose number corresponds with the number shown by the dice. The cat with the highest number begins by throwing both dice and moving the relevant number of squares. Once past square 108, only one dice should be used.

2 If a player lands on a square in which the cat Ronron is shown climbing up a ladder, he proceeds to the top of it. If, on the other hand, the player reaches a square whence the tomcat Ronron is forced to take flight, he must descend to the square at the foot of the ladder.

3 Because of this combination of ups and downs, it may easily happen that a player who has nearly reached his goal lands on 104 and suddenly has to go all the way back to 21, while another player who was far behind surges ahead to win unexpectedly. The player who first reaches (or passes) 120 WINS the game.

Kilkenny Cats

Parker Brothers of Salem, Massachusetts, were the publishers of the *Amusing Game of Kilkenny Cats* which they copyrighted in 1890 and which they kept in their catalogue for many years. It was inspired by the popular poem on the two cats from Kilkenny.

> There once were two cats in Kilkenny,
> Each thought there was one cat too many;
> They scratched and they bit, they clawed and they fit,
> Till, – excepting their nails, and the tips of their tails,
> Instead of two cats, – there weren't any!

RULES OF PLAY

1 This is a game for two, three, or four players. Each player has eight cats of one colour which he lines up on the eight kitten heads. The game is played with one dice. The object of the game is to be the first to place a cat on each of the two mice squares opposite to one's opening line-up.

2 Players throw the dice which represents 'Fickle Fortune' and move in turn. On throwing the dice, a player may move one of his cats as many spaces as is shown on the dice face in one straight line: backwards or forwards, left, right, or diagonally. The cat may not pass by or jump over another cat in its path; however, if a cat lands on a square occupied by another cat, he removes it from the board.

3 We must CAUTION each player to keep in mind that his object is to be the first to fill his two mice squares, and, while waging Kilkenny fights is exciting, indulging in too many may prove a self-defeating pastime.

4 No player is allowed to move his cats on to any mouse square but his own, and once moved on to a mouse square, a piece cannot be moved again. The mice squares must be reached by an exact throw so that, if a player no longer has other cats to move, and his throw would take him beyond the mouse square, he must instead move the cat in some other direction.

5 Whoever first succeeds in filling his two mice squares WINS the game.

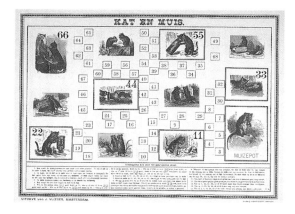

Kattepot-Muizepot

Kattepot-Muizepot was issued in Amsterdam between 1885 and 1890 under the title of *Kat en Muise* (Cat and Mouse). It was printed by 'Senefelder' and published by N. Nieger. The pictures on the board are taken from the works of three leading illustrators: the English artists Alfred Elwes and Harrison Weir, and the American Palmer Cox.

It is a gambling game for two players and requires two dice, two counters and chips—or money. The stakes are unlimited by anything except the players' inclination—or ability—to pay.

RULES OF PLAY

1 The players take it in turn to throw both dice. The player with the higher score becomes Cat; the other, Mouse. They put the agreed stakes in the pots: Cat in her Kattepot on red 66 and Mouse in his Muizepot on black 66. Cat moves to the top left-hand corner of the board and Mouse to the bottom right.

2 Cat begins the game by throwing both dice and preparing to move her counter along the Cat Walk—the red numbered squares—to square 3 if the dice show 2 and 1, square 4 if they show 3 and 1, square 5 if they show 2 and 3 or 4 and 1, and so on. If Cat throws a double 1 she moves to square 11, in which case Mouse must pay her two chips. If she throws a double 6 she pays two chips to Mouse and does not move. If she lands on 5 she loses her next turn, but if she lands on 10 she may throw again; if she lands on 4 or 9 she pays one chip to Mouse.

3 Mouse now throws and moves in the same way down the Mouse Run—the black numbered squares—paying or receiving the same number of chips. ▶

4 Cat's turn again, and the same rules apply. But there are more: if Cat has to jump her counter over Mouse's, she pays him one chip; if she lands on square 15 she loses her next turn; square 20 gives her a second throw; and 16 means another chip paid to Mouse. If she is already past square 11 by this turn, a double 2 will take her to square 22 – otherwise it is only the total 4 that counts. If she lands on square 22, Mouse must pay her two chips.

5 Mouse follows Cat, and Cat then follows Mouse again, each racing for the other's pot on square 66. The earlier rules still apply: landing on 22, 33, 44 or 55 earns two chips; once past 22 a double 3 leads straight to square 33, and once past 33 two 4s lead to 44 and past that two 5s to 55. Once past 55 a double six is a passport straight to the pot. Before that a double 6 still means a lost turn and a forfeit of two chips to the other player. Landing on squares 25, 35, 45 or 65 means a lost turn, while achieving squares 30, 40, 50 or 60 gains a second throw; stopping on 25, 36, 49 or 64 entails paying over one chip to the other player.

6 If Cat or Mouse throws a total which will take him or her beyond square 66, he or she has to turn back to 48. But the player who reaches 66 first WINS the game and takes both stakes.

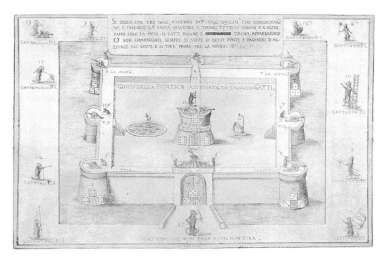

La Pontica

The Italian dice game *Il Gioco della Pontica* (The Game of the Drawbridge) is a variation of the more famous *Il Gioco della Barca* (The Boat Game), which is played with only two dice. The decorative board for *La Pontica*, engraved by Bulino and showing a castle defended by brave mice and besieged by determined cats, was issued by F. M. Mitelli in 1690. It is a forgotten classic which modern gamblers will find as compelling as did those who first hazarded their fortunes trying to cross the drawbridge nearly three centuries ago.

RULES OF PLAY

1 First the players must decide on the stakes and pay them into the bank. Then, each in turn (and this is a game which can be played by any number) throws three dice. The player with the highest score becomes the banker and has the privilege of making the first throw of the game.

2 Starting with the banker, the players, in clockwise order, cast the dice. The total shown by the dice will correspond to one of the aggressive cats or one of the brave mice on the board, and the player either pays into the bank or receives from it a proportion of the stakes. The most highly favoured scores are the triples – three 1s, 2s, 3s and so on – which represent the mice. All but two of the attacking cats have to pay into the bank, but 17, known as Gattone, is neutral, neither paying nor taking. ▶

3 The amounts to be paid or collected are as follows:

  3 (three 1s) collects half the stakes
4 collects three stakes
5 Gattazzo pays three stakes
6 Gattuzzo pays two stakes

  6 (three 2s) collects half the stakes
7 collects three stakes
8 Gattarotto pays three stakes
9 Gattetto pays one stake

  9 (three 3s) collects half the stakes
10 Gattotto pays two stakes
11 collects three stakes
12 Gattino pays one stake

12 (three 4s) collects half the stakes
13 Gattarello pays one stake
14 Gatto pays one stake
15 Gattoncello pays one stake

15 (three 5s) collects half the stakes
16 Gattarino pays one stake
17 Gattone does not pay and does not collect

18 (three 6s) collects all of the stakes in the bank.